To Joyce!

Please enjoy this
in good health.

Love!
Gigi 12·19·10

Dedicated to my grandchildren:

Aden, Hannah and Aaryl

Acknowledgments

My first acknowledgment goes to Pima Community College, who awarded me a sabbatical and opportunity to do this book, which I am so grateful for. I am just so glad they believed in me.

My dear friend, Aryen Hart, artist extraordinaire, without his persistence and reminders of, "Oh sure you can do it", back in 2001, I might not have even started the whole process. All my family, first my son, Adam Brown, who says it like it is and is always my guiding light; my sister Brenda Thomas, who makes me look good and feel great; my brother Hal Davis, who has been a mentor and confident; and especially my mother, "Ginger" Carter, who also told me I would, and should do this book.

My deep appreciation goes to Beth Showalter, my illustrator and friend. Definitely, without her beautiful drawings, great ideas and wonderful collaboration, this book would just not be. She was a past student, in interior design and I must say, one of the very best. She is so talented.

Next, I would like to mention my editor and good friend, Christine Erkman. Goodness, she just plowed through all my writing and it was wonderful. She is a graduate student, in interior design, and again, one of the best.

I also would very much like to thank the people who read though my book and made suggestions, particularly, Janet Wootten, Valeria La Master, and Dorothy Gyurko.

Also, many thanks to, Will Foster, PhD, who read it though, red-lined and encouraged me, by saying, "This is really good".

CONTENTS

INTRODUCTION

I believe the time has come to seek out and create your own personal sanctuary space. The whole world seems to be spinning out of control with ongoing threats of terrorism, globalization, and the overwhelming array of communications technologies available 24-hours a day. Our lives and our world seem hectic and stressful and allocating "down" time is even more important now than ever before. Life does not always give us a nurturing environment. As information overload threatens to swamp us, employers now recognize the need to create spaces where workers can temporarily escape the madness. Today's world can seem particularly threatening to our personal space. We can become upset and even withdrawn. Therefore, your sanctuary space must be a place where you can disconnect from some worldly things and begin to nourish and build your inner strength and wisdom.

All members of a household or a work place need their own space where they can entirely be themselves, free from disturbances.

- David Pearson, architect and author of *The Natural House Book*

This book will help you design and create a sanctuary for yourself.

Everyone has a need for privacy and personal space to some degree. We all need time away from others, somewhere to replenish our spirit, to find stillness. Space is required to accomplish that, even in your own mind. Your sanctuary space may or may not be completely separated from all distractions, depending on your situation, but you can define this space to be a retreat from stress.

Writing this book was something that I thought about for many years. It is filled with practical information, guidance, and inspiring ideas to help you create your sanctuary space.

The contents will help you plan for a sanctuary in your home, workplace, or wherever you travel. Interior design fundamentals will help you visualize the concepts and exercises will guide you in your endeavors. Once established, you may find that your sanctuary needs minor adjustments now and then. As it develops, the most important thing to keep in mind is to fill your sanctuary with love and let yourself relax.

In order to help others, I also had to go through this process. It's often much easier to help others than to help yourself. I had difficulty organizing, clearing needless stuff out of my way, and it affected my interior design business. There were moments when I thought there was no light at the end of that self-made tunnel. Clearing away the debris is a wonderful, uplifting experience. Creating something as important as your own personal sanctuary will take some time, a little patience, and staying focused on your goal. What does sanctuary means to you? What is the purpose of creating one? As we walk through the many stages of life, I believe that our environments, especially the interior spaces, can help calm and recharge our souls. Your sanctuary space can be a source of joyful personal refreshment within your special surroundings. When you enter, you will leave all cares and worries at the threshold. Time in this space will belong to you alone, a place where the world fades... your sanctuary.

Having some space of one's own in the home is fundamental to balanced relations within a couple or a family. A person's own bedroom or study or work place permits him to seek privacy, to make it clear to others that he or she needs time alone.

- Psychologist Clara Cooper Marcus

Gigi

Gigi Davis Brown

HOW TO USE THIS BOOK

You'll find many "What To Do" exercises, all of them leading you closer and closer to your perfect sanctuary space. Use as many of the exercises as you wish and take notes in a journal. Through your journal, your sanctuary will begin to materialize before your mind's eye. Once visualized, it will be a short road towards achieving your sanctuary space.

Organize Your Thoughts The best way to fully benefit from the guidance you'll find in this book is to keep a journal, literally a book of blank pages with sufficient space to write your thoughts and impressions.

What To Do

- Save magazine photos, fabric clippings, and other samples; paste them in your journal or add a pocket page to store them.
- Create a list of questions about your initial ideas for your sanctuary; as you gather information and arrive at the answers, jot them down.
- List some goals, both short-term and long-term.
- Leave space to draw or sketch if you're inclined to do so.
- Write about your dreams; they may contain messages about your sanctuary.
- Practice visualizing what you want to create.

Keeping a journal will open up your subconscious to what you really want in your sanctuary space, to what really inspires you spiritually, in the direction you wish to point your spiritual self in your everyday life.

All of us, whether man or woman, child or adult, in a relationship or not, **need a place we can call our own***, at the very least, a place where we can shut the door from time to time and know we will not be disturbed.*

- Jane Alexander, author of
Spirit of the Home

Your sanctuary at home or workplace can be any room or part of a room...

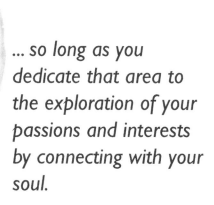

... so long as you dedicate that area to the exploration of your passions and interests by connecting with your soul.

CHAPTER ONE: SANCTUARY

WHAT IS SANCTUARY?

The word sanctuary itself derives from the Latin word for sacred. It has several other meanings; retreat, altar, shrine, church and sanctum. Every civilization on every continent possesses its own version, both in myth and in actuality. The Encyclopedia Britannica records that, "a temple implies a sanctuary, but, a sanctuary does not necessarily contain a temple". Therefore, sanctuary has many meanings. The important question is: What does it mean to you?

Sanctuary means different things to different people as well as to different cultures.

Here is a quote from one of my former students. Her kind of sanctuary: "is a safe and quiet place where I can be alone (very important); no radio, no TV, no phones, no computer...no modern electronics; preferably, with my cats, surrounded by plants, the waterfall trickling, a cup of hot tea (or a glass of wine), and an interesting book. Sometimes, my backyard is my sanctuary. I enjoy just walking around watering the plants, inspecting and caring for them. Other times, it's a room in my house. The key ingredients are: 1) alone 2) no electronics 3) with cats. It helps me rest, relax and rejuvenate. It might only be an hour, or maybe it's all day. Regardless, I feel more centered and ready to deal with my relationships, my work, and life in general".

Your sanctuary may be a place of quiet and peace; a place devoted to reading or practicing yoga; journal writing; meditation; whatever pleases you. It doesn't matter which room or space in your house you choose, as long as it has the potential to provide you with what you need for your sanctuary. We each have individual needs. You're looking for that place where you and no one else can be happiest.

Don't worry if you lack the space to dedicate an entire room to your sanctuary. Most of us don't have a completely empty room that could be devoted just to sanctuary space. Look around your home or workplace critically.

What To Do

- Stand inside your home or workplace with your back to the front door. Imagine you are entering for the first time.
- Walk around checking out small areas of each room; perhaps some areas can be made to feel or appear to be apart from it.

What space is unused? What can you claim? Can spaces such as a guestroom, dining room, den, basement, attic, or even garage be used? How about a porch or patio area?
One thing we might all agree on is a feeling of safety in a sanctuary. A sanctuary should be a safe place with a sense of divinity. Sanctuary should be a place of reflection, a place to dream without boundaries, away from the stress of the world. Basically, it is a personal privacy refuge, safe and secure. What does sanctuary really mean for you? What restores your power, hope, and psychological stability? Could it be your favorite chair and a good book? Might you think of gardens, reflecting pools, fountains and the comforting sounds of spilling water? Perhaps your sanctuary is one of total silence. Do you think of a spa, where the body and soul receive equal and tender treatment? There are endless possibilities for your personal sanctuary: sitting quietly; focusing on a cluster of trees; walking on a path; listening to the sounds of a babbling brook; watching the slow patterns of shadows or clouds. Think of what symbols immediately convey to you that a space is a sanctuary.

INSPIRATION

What inspires you? I find myself inspired by travel, nature, and sometime by details that people seldom see. I love doors and, in many of my travels, I take photos of different types of doors. I like to photograph the details of architecture. Nature has always been a source of inspiration. It's easy to love nature and almost everyone can be inspired and appreciate the beauty of the outdoors. The dramatic thrill of a storm with thunder and lightning can be exciting. How can we bring this inspiration to work for you indoors?

The inspired 'designer' will observe the universe, absorbing impressions from all their experiences.

What To Do
- Take a nature walk or hike.
- Seek out things that amaze you, inspire you, or calm you.
- Allow yourself some quiet time.

INTENTION

We understand intention to be something we purposely do. As an interior designer, my intention would be to plan an objective, create a design (concepts and drawings), and take the necessary action to fulfill the objective. You will essentially do the same thing to create your sanctuary.

The single largest pool of untapped resource in this world is human good intentions that never translate into action.

— Cindy Gallop

First, let us recognize the power of intention and what it means to you. What do you want to attract into your space? Identify your intentions. Conjure it up in your mind and in your heart. This will be your starting place. Your final result may not be exactly as you initially conceived, but identifying your intentions could bring about the perfect solutions.

What to do:
- Check in your emotions
- Dare to dream. Dream big.
- Sit quietly, uninterrupted; breathe slowly and release the stress of the day.
- Be aware of the space around you.
- Imagine how you would like the space to be; imagine the most exquisite details, in full-blown color.
- Imagine the scents; visualize the textures and how the textures feel; imagine the views and any sounds.
- Write down your thoughts in your journal, even to the smallest detail.
- Make a collage using all of the photos, samples, etc. You may do this any way you feel like doing it.
- By taking these small steps and inventing your sanctuary space in your mind, you are using your intentions to guide you towards the best decisions.

Emotions reflect intentions. Therefore, awareness of emotions leads to awareness of intentions.

- Gary Zukav

LISTENING

You can replenish yourself and fully enjoy your space
simply by listening. Listening may require slowing
down from the usual pace. It is especially important to
listen to your inner voice, your spirit. Spirit will help you
understand and create your sanctuary. As your sanctuary
develops, you, your life and physical surroundings will
change. From this book, you will begin to develop skills
to be intuitive, to become a better listener, and gain a
better understanding of yourself. By listening to your
spirit, that inner voice will create greater awareness of your
environment.

Your home has plenty to say to you; so does your work
place. This may be more difficult because there are
distractions, disturbances, and perhaps interruptions. On
top of this, it could be hard to find the time or place for
stillness. Once you've accomplished this very first task, you
will begin to understand what is needed in the process of
creating your sanctuary.

Listening is simply the beginning.

*So, when you are listening to somebody or thing,
completely, attentively, then you are listening
not only to the words or sounds, but also to the
feeling of what is being conveyed, to the whole
of it, not part of it.*

— Jiddu Krishnamurti

What To Do:

- Slow down and listen.
- Pay close attention.
- Imagine your heart has ears.
- Sit quietly in the space you set aside for your sanctuary. If you're not sure where the space will be, it's okay to begin your listening in any space.
- Ideas come to you through your thoughts during those quiet moments.
- Some gentle self-questioning is most likely the very thing you should try with yourself.
- Examine, probe, and analyze the space where you are sitting.
- Record your thoughts in your journal for review at a later time.

REMODELING OR NEW CONSTRUCTION

Eventually, after the listening, meditation, cleaning, and clearing, you will want to move things around, painting, adding or taking away items. Consider starting small, changing your space and items as often as you feel necessary. What felt good yesterday may not feel the same way today. Feel free to change, re-arrange, remodel or build new. Do whatever you need to do.

Like yourself, your spirit grows and you will evolve.

CHANGING YOUR STUFF

My friend changes her sanctuary area (a little space at the end of her kitchen bar countertop) quite often, because her needs change.

One day it will have a photo of a couple and their wedding invitation, along with fresh flowers from her garden, a beautiful scented candle and other trinkets and memorabilia. The next week, it changes to another theme. You get the idea. We are all unique and you might find yourself doing things differently than any of my suggestions. This is as it should be. You will find many suggestions throughout this book which should help you raise your awareness and consciousness to the limitless ways of creating sanctuary.

Each reader must create a space according to their own specific needs and beliefs. The material in this book will help create and maintain your sanctuary as you evolve through life. Take all the time you need to study the exercises. Keep in mind that you will be acting with intention, acting in alignment with your higher selves, but most of all, acting with the power of love and commitment to your sanctuary.

SYMBOLS AND SYMBOLISM

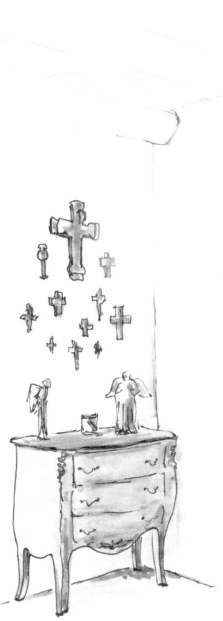

What is a symbol? A symbol is something that is used to represent a concept, such as a deity; a tangible thing like lightning or an intangible thing, such as thunder. Symbols often imply great or mystical power. Symbols have been used by mankind for thousands of years and continue to be a very important part of our daily lives. A logo or an emblem can trigger strong emotions. We're flooded with symbols every day, such as:

> Lion = bravery, courage, king of the jungle
> The crucifix = Christianity, sacrifice, Jesus
> Dove = peace, hope
> Shamrock = Ireland, luck, Saint Patrick's day

The symbols around you may activate or influence your behavior. They can trigger relaxation and hope or apprehension and distrust. You may currently be subjected to conflicting environmental messages or to symbolic information that undermines your being. Therefore, your choice of symbols for your sanctuary will be important to reflect the best in you. Minimize those symbols that decrease your vitality. Used consciously, symbolism can be a powerful tool to help you extract what you will need for your sanctuary.

Symbols are intimate connections, whether you are conscious of them or not.

Symbols often embody relationships or connections that we might otherwise miss. Watch your reactions to symbols for clues. At first, it may not be easy; you may be overwhelmed by all the incoming symbols and associated messages. With practice, you will become more sensitive to symbolism and environmental messages. You will then be able to identify and eliminate the things around you that raise negative responses. Instead, emphasize symbols of happiness and continuity of life. For example: What things or qualities mean love to you? Do you react positively to certain colors, shapes, textures, smells and sounds? What connotes security, peacefulness, and order? Do you need to connect with nature? (There's that nature thing again!)

For the present, we will presume that most of us do not have trees growing inside our homes or babbling brooks meandering through our workplaces. What kinds of things can you do to simulate a natural setting? Begin by looking for symbols and icons to help bring a representation of nature into your sanctuary. These symbols and icons can be elements of design along with natural elements to create themes.

For example, a private corner that can afford emotional release; a bench (furniture) which can hint at contemplative peace; colors (design element) that can alter our moods, such as blue for a calm feeling; and, textures (design element) that can give softness and comfort to you. Again, all of this will depend on your exact needs and wants. Exploring your feelings and insights will guide you through the different design aspects. Your actions will dictate the design of this space. Ask yourself: What restores my power, hope, and psychological stability while using this space? Symbolic actions are essential ingredients in the human understanding of sacred space.

The all-important purpose of a sanctuary space is to help you feel good.

What To Do:

- List the sacred qualities you want in your life. Think about what symbols you associate with each one. If you realize that connection is with the earth, you might want earth materials around you: a stone floor, bricks, clay, or terra-cotta pots. If you want to make a place for relaxation, you might use calming colors, water, peaceful music and a few beautiful natural objects.

- Use the power of positive symbolic messages that mean something to you in your special space.

- Link with your heritage. List symbols from your roots, traditions, and cultural aspects of your life. Your roots are a great way to bring a sense of being solidly grounded, inner strength, and resilience into your life. Look to your culture, your lifestyle, your path and see if they provide meaning for you. When you have identified these meaningful symbols, place them in an area where you will often see them. Situating these objects in clear view is a very effective reminder of your sanctuary feelings.

- A symbol that has been intentionally selected for your sacred space will be a silent affirmation of your fondest dreams.

IMAGES AND OBJECTS

Objects chosen to surround you will contribute in a very real way to your feeling of well being; **they will also speak to your soul.**

Images come from your thoughts and are like symbols. Objects, which can be powerful from many standpoints, speak directly to the soul and can bring up intense, often forgotten emotions. Think about what happens when you pick up something connected with your past, or find a similar item to something you remember from your childhood. Memories may come flooding back. Often, you feel overwhelmed by the force of your past and the strength of your emotions.

Objects carry a charge. They can have deep and meaningful resonance for you. Yet, many of the things with which we fill our spaces are somehow dead and strangely lifeless. They fill a gap or provide a bit of color, but what do they do for your spirit? Objects of the soul come in many strange forms and only you will recognize them for what they represent.

You don't have to prowl the world to find some true crafts. My friends and I have found the most beautiful objects for our homes in second-hand stores and thrift shops. They may even have been picked up for just a few pennies at a yard sale. They can give immense pleasure to you over many years, regardless of their material value. I also love to look for Native American pottery and baskets, African carvings and cloth, and paintings of all kinds. There are communities still using traditional low-tech materials to produce beautiful things with soul. Some of my very favorite objects in my home are from Mexico. Italian pottery also has an honest, earthy quality. Think of a perfectly turned wooden bowl with a rich resinous scent. Willow baskets are useful, highly practical, and visually appealing. What would you think about the clean lines of a Shaker chair, a homespun hand-stitched quilt, or a woven Persian rug?

Don't take a shopping list and expect to find everything in one trip. Do keep an open mind and think about images and objects for your sanctuary space that connect with your soul. These are things that you will accumulate over a period of time or a lifetime. No one can dictate which item will connect with your soul. Only you can decide this for yourself.

I look for things that are hand crafted, lovingly made, with a wealth of history attached to them.

What To Do:

- Try arranging a collection of items, all of the same type to make an interesting display. Before you begin, make sure you choose a theme that strikes a chord deep within you. How about a candle collection?
- Look around your home to see what items and objects really mean something to your soul. Sometimes, these items are hiding in a basement or stored in an attic or shed.
- If they are from a past time you wish to forget, it may be best to just get rid of them.
- Surround yourself with things that reflect your personality.
- Go "junking" to the thrift store, as I like to call it.

MOBILE SANCTUARY

When I travel, especially if I will be away for a long time, I like to take a small statue of St. Francis of Assisi with me. The statue is stored inside a beautifully decorated 3" x 4" box with little French doors that open. It also contains some of his prayers which I use as affirmations during meditation. Once opened, the statue can be stood next to the box like a mini church and can be taken anywhere.

I have a dear friend who has a little Buddha statue hanging from her rearview mirror in her car. When she returned from a trip to Bali, she brought one for me. I have it hanging just outside my front door from a beautiful handmade cross. Some people place small statues of Jesus on the dash or console of their car. Others hang crystals of all shapes, colors, and sizes from the rear view mirror. Another friend has a dream catcher hanging in her car. Some people like to carry photos of loved ones in wallets or purses, while others carry prayers or pictures of saints or angels.

There may be times when the only place you can get a little time alone is in your car. Having a little reminder of your sanctuary might help remove some of your daily stress. I think of my car as a refuge from work, although I don't even have to drive anywhere.

If I need some time to just sit alone, I can meditate in my car in the parking lot or drive to a nearby park for a refreshing break.

What To Do:

- Take along an item which can help you achieve your sanctuary mood.
- Carry personal items in your car, purse or wallet to use for inspiration and a sense of sanctuary.

LIFESTYLE

What are your roles in life? How do you play them? See what you can come up with. Besides being a teacher, computer analyst, nurse, mother/father, wife/husband, sister/brother, daughter/son, aunt/uncle, cousin or friend, you maybe also a cook, gardener, poet, dog walker, or even a quilt-maker. Everyone plays many roles throughout their lifetime. It's good for you to know all your lifestyles and how that can work in the creation of a sanctuary space.

See if you can find a place in your house that reflects your roles. What roles would you like to express more? Where do you spend the most time in your home? The least? Where would you like to spend more time?

Look for areas of your house that may be missing some of your essence.

What To Do:

- Try and answer some of these questions.
- Write down in your journal all the roles you've had in life. Then list all the ones you play now. Which role is the largest? Which roles are the least?
- Draw a circle and divide it into segments. Label each segment to represent the amount of time you devote to each role.
- Within each segment, note how that role that pertains to you; for example, work or business; home; garden; family; friends; school; hobby; charity; spiritual, and so on.
- Draw another circle, but divide the segments the way you would really like it to be. This could represent your ideal lifestyle.

Once you've identified your ideal lifestyle, you can begin to change these elements and other items in your home to help achieve your sanctuary.

POSITIVE THINKING

When creating sanctuary, you should not feel restricted or limited in your thinking.

Think positively. This can hold fast and true when being creative because you are what you think. You are your thoughts and it will be important to stay positively focused while you're creating your sanctuary space. "Good attitude is… well…everything."

What To Do:
- Meditate on the reality that what we choose and how our egos deal with it. It is a matter of choice.
- Recite this little prayer:
     "God, grant me the serenity to accept the things
     I cannot change, the courage to change the
     things I can, and the wisdom to know the difference."
- Try thinking with gratitude. There is usually someone who is in a more difficult situation than you.

CHAPTER TWO: ELEMENTS & PRINCIPLES

The principles and elements of design are tools to help you create your sanctuary. I like to think of the elements as ingredients and the principles as a combined mixture of ingredients that make any design. You may inject an element, such as color or texture, to create harmony, balance, rhythm, scale and proportion. The interrelationship of elements and principles combined with your personal inspirations and responses will result in a space that is uniquely your own. Nature is one of the best teachers for observing principles and elements in design. Keep this in mind as you create your space and it will help guide you.

ELEMENT OF SPACE

The element of space includes positive and negative aspects. Physically, the positive space is the furniture and anything else that takes up the actual or three-dimensional space. Negative space is the open space for movement.

Your sanctuary space can be part of a room, like a bedroom, or a space designated specifically as your sanctuary. Allow for some movement within the space and arrange your furniture to strike the balance between the positive and negative space. An atmosphere of safety and comfort is important, too. Physical things will transform your space into a sanctuary setting that suits your needs and revives your spirit.

Negative space is just as important as the positive space for all things to function well.

What To Do:

- Use pencil, pen, crayon, or whatever medium you prefer to sketch out some plans for your space, such as a furniture layout.
- Refer back to your collection of magazine photos for examples and ideas.
- Draw any details you envision in your sanctuary.
- If you have difficulty visualizing the space, string up a clothesline and hang fabric around an area to create an enclosed space.

FUNCTION AND CONSTRAINTS OF SPACE

Understand your needs, exercise your choices, and stay true to your heart.

The most important feature of your space will be its function. Dissatisfaction or unhappiness with your sanctuary space can usually be traced back to your preliminary decision making. Careful planning may help to avoid any problems. There may be some architectural consideration or other constraints that seem overwhelming when designing your space. Approach them as challenges and, in many cases, these issues can help make your tasks easier. You may not be able to change things, so accept that and be guided by your constraints. Your most intimate and personal desires are found in your heart. Plan for function and design for your pleasure; you will want to return to it again and again.

INTEGRITY OF SPACE

Good design integrity combines your concept, its execution, and the final outcome. Integrity starts with considering the best materials to use in that space, availability of those materials, and their durability. Consider any health aspects of your materials, such as formaldehyde in the furniture.

ACTUAL SPACE

It doesn't matter how small it is, you can always find ways to help pursue your goal of sanctuary. This could require a shift of rooms or functions of space. For example, your home office might be better hidden in the dining room with its lively atmosphere than in your bedroom where you retreat and relax. You might be able to create some space by hanging fabric, blinds, or screens. The ideal situation is to have a designated room for your sanctuary. If that can't be, explore some areas of your home or workplace for sanctuary space.

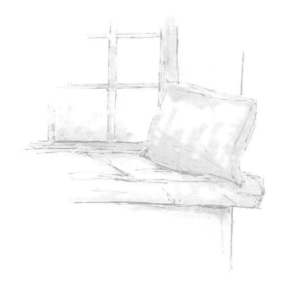

Is there a place you can sit quietly or curl up in a chair and gaze out a window?

Bedroom

If you cannot dedicate a separate area or room in your home for your sanctuary space, my first choice would be the bedroom. This is because it is usually a quiet place. A bedroom can often be where you can find rest and tranquility away from the family.

You will want to create a definite relaxation area, perhaps in a corner of the room near a window. You may want to screen this area from the rest of the room with a decorative divider or some plants. Avoid overcrowding the space but try to keep it organized by using small cupboards or shelving. Allow plenty of air and energy to flow throughout the space.

Bathroom

This area of the house is sometimes the only place in which family members can retreat and lock the door for privacy. The bathroom can be a good place for your sanctuary, especially if you are not rushed and can be given the time you need.

Let's assume the bathroom is your designated sanctuary. What can you do to make it feel more like a sanctuary? It can be very challenging if your bathroom is small. Mirrors can work miracles for small and challenging spaces. Mirrors reflect the space and make it appear much larger.

A natural light source to brighten the space is also helpful. Not only will natural light be healing, but it will make it the room seem larger. Hopefully, you will be able to open a window to let in the fresh air. Fresh air is most important for good health and well being. Naturally, this should be a primary factor for your sanctuary.

Using natural products and materials in a bathroom will create a restful and relaxing space. Warm and soothing colors make you feel more comfortable and will encourage

Place a comfortable chair and small table where you can enjoy breakfast or a cup of tea.

you to linger in your bathroom. Along those lines, choose colors that make you feel good and look even better.

Another item to consider for a bathroom sanctuary is aroma. Candles, incense, scented soaps, bath powders, and bath salts in scents that you love will help you relax and unwind.

Finally, we mustn't forget to include something from nature. Plants can be a wonderful addition in bathrooms. You might find that it's easier to take care of plants in bathrooms where there's plenty of moisture.

Flowering plants often have a subtle perfume that can enhance your sense of sanctuary in the bath.

Kitchens and Dining Rooms

Although it may seem an unlikely place for sanctuary, your kitchen or dining room could be right for you. Maybe you can create a niche in front of a crackling fireplace. Perhaps you gravitate to a dining or kitchen table; guests always seem to gather in the kitchen, so it may be a perfectly acceptable sanctuary spot. Every home needs an area where family and friends can gather in a place both comfortable and mellow. There may be a time, however, that it should be for you and you alone. In this situation, you may have to consider the entire space as a whole sanctuary. Most people spend many hours in their kitchen environment. A well-designed kitchen may be functional, but it can also be an attractive and appealing space.

Make your kitchen or dining area into a holistic environment by considering all aspects of the space.

First, consider your floors. You will be spending a lot of time in your kitchen or dining room. Your flooring can make a great difference as to whether you come away worn out and tired or relaxed and ready to enjoy the remainder of your day or evening. Wood is perhaps one of your best choices for a sanctuary. Wood is natural, warm, earthy, and inviting. Another natural product which can be used is linoleum. Carpeting is a good choice for a dining room, but not a kitchen where a natural fiber area rug on a tile floor might be a better choice. One of my kitchens (I have two) has a clay tile floor. Clay is a natural product, but very hard, noisy to walk on, and feels cold. To help with the comfort and noise levels,

I recently placed a large sisal grass mat on the floor. There is new interest in bamboo flooring which is offered in several lovely colors, durable, and good for the environment.

Second, make sure your furniture is comfortable. Not only will you be spending a lot of time standing in your kitchen or dining room, you may be spending equal time sitting.

I remember visiting a friend who had just purchased a new dining set. They were so comfortable that we ended up spending hours there, even after we cleared the remnants of our dinner from the table. Because it was such a pleasant experience, I can clearly recall that the chairs were upholstered in a nice tightly woven but soft wool fabric. The chairs had casters that could be locked, if needed. All of the chairs had arms and, best of all, they leaned back and rocked! The table was beautifully polished oak, with a round top and a pedestal base.

The fact is: if you're comfortable in your space, you will want to be there with friends, family or simply alone.

Living room

Part or all of your living room can be a place for your sanctuary, but it depends on your circumstances. In fact, my living room is not a room where we live. It does not have a TV, but it does have music, some extremely comfortable furniture, and fabulous natural lighting and airflow. This space is an ideal sanctuary space and I can use it for that purpose, if I choose. There are many spaces in my home for sanctuary, even in my office. Earlier, I mentioned that I needed to create sanctuary in my home in order to begin writing this book to help others do the same. Therefore, I created many areas of my home for sanctuary and my goal is to make my entire home into a sanctuary space.

If you have a fireplace in your living room, the hearth is considered the heart of a home and is quite often the focal point of that space. It's also great for gazing and meditating. Perhaps you have a beautiful view from your living room that brings in natural light and warmth. With this in mind, the living room can be a wonderful place for relaxing, for daydreaming, and peace.

The use of natural materials is always encouraged.

Workspace or Home Office Space

In your home office or study, your desk or workstation is the most powerful piece of furniture. If possible, it should be in the most powerful position. Your back should not face the door, nor should you be in direct line with the door. You should be situated so that you have visual domain of the room. This also gives you some security and makes your space safer for you.

Keep your furniture simple and don't clutter the space with lots of stuff.

If you like to have things close by, store them in closets or on shelves. Avoid busy patterns in an office sanctuary as they could be distracting. To increase mental stimulation, introduce subtle contrasts in fabrics. Try using contrasting colors in earth hues, such as soft shade of beiges, creams and browns, or contrasting textures. These suggestions for an office sanctuary will help you get started and you'll soon discover what will work best for you.

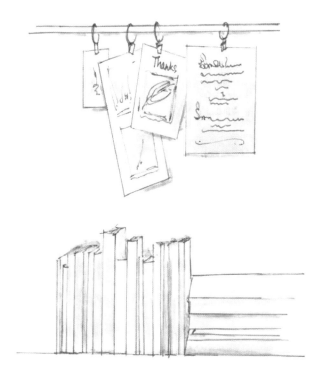

The more successful you are in reflecting your personality in your home workplace, the more you will gravitate toward it.

People choose to work at home, not simply out of necessity but because it allows them to be something they cannot be in a corporate office. For this reason, decorating the home office is an exercise in self-expression. Personalize your home workspace with inspirational photos, artwork, or awards, and take ownership of those many work hours.

ELEMENT OF SHAPE

Shapes are a very human aspect of life: human beings come in all shapes and sizes.

We define our human shape as a natural form. When we want things around us to be safe and non-threatening, we should consider shapes of softness and curves. Shapes are also symbolic of feelings. A circle, representing eternity, has no beginning or end. Most of us live in a box with four walls, a floor, and a ceiling. When you have to live inside a box-like shape, those walls, ceilings and floors can feel like they are closing in around you. I live in an adobe house shaped like a long rectangle. Living in the Southwest, I have many opportunities to have my windows and doors open at least half the year.

What To Do:
- Think in fluid terms, contour lines, and flowing shapes.
- Consider placement of decorative designs (using positive space) as well negative space to create shapes.
- Vaulted ceilings, skylights, windows, and doors can make a room seem more spacious, avoiding the feeling of being boxed in.

ELEMENT OF COLOR

Color has the power to lift our spirits, to soothe our souls, to enliven us or calm us.

All design elements are important, but the one that gets the most attention is color. This element is just plain fun, can be very affordable, and make huge differences in your space. The colors we choose can enormously affect our lives. This element is very much connected to our emotions.

Using nature as a starting point, look around you and pick out the colors which really make your soul sing. A variety of flowers would be a wonderful palette to consider; the autumn leaves in their blaze of yellow, gold, red, and brown; or, a cloudless blue sky. I love the sea, especially, the Caribbean, with all its values and shades of blue. Think about oceans and mountains at sunrise or sunset. There is an entire spectrum of incredible colors to play with that will work for you.

Colors can relate to the physical, social, and psychological aspects of our lives. Color can be symbolic and the symbolism can vary from culture to culture. In Feng Shui, certain colors are more auspicious (very good), such as red and orange. Other colors relate to the five elements: water, fire, earth, metal and wood.

What are your favorite colors and what effects do they have on you? What emotions do they bring to mind? Try to imagine decorating and creating your sanctuary with colors. Try to envision how all the colors can help you achieve your goals.

Play with colors, have fun with them, experiment. A faux finish painter reminded me: "If you don't like it, you can change it." Just see what pleases your eyes. Stay tuned in to your intuition and sense of color. There are an unlimited number of different shades and tones. You aren't limited

"I found I could say things with color and shapes that I couldn't say any other way - things I had no words for."

- Georgia O'Keeffe

to the primary colors or pastels. Generally, the space will need a combination of colors to create a sense of harmony. Use your intuition to gauge the balance of color in relation to the furnishings and yourself.

What To Do

- Take yourself window shopping; fashion is all around.
- Stay away from trendy things and look for colors that make you happy.
- Build a library of colors by collecting color charts or paint strip samples.
- Go to several fabric stores and get samples of fabric with colors and textures you like.
- Take your color samples home and arrange them on a table; study how the colors and textures look in different light; rearrange them and note any changes.
- Buy small jars of paint to experiment with various paint colors.
- On a poster board, layout your favorite paint samples and fabrics; move them around until you are happy with the combinations.
- Try some different color schemes; for example, all one color, but with different textures or tone-on-tone patterns (monochromatic) or colors that are opposites (complementary), such as red & green, blue & orange, or violet & yellow.
- If you are feeling unsure, seek out help from a color consultant.

ELEMENT OF LIGHT

Light is perhaps one of the most important elements of design and is probably one of the most neglected. We take light for granted. Without light, we cannot see. Light produces life. Light influences our perception of colors and textures and our moods. General lighting is used to soften shadows, smooth out and expand corners, or provide a comfortable level for safety and maintenance.

When planning your sanctuary, consider the lighting very carefully. Natural lighting is best because it is the most healing, although, not always reliable or even practical. Artificial lighting will be the utmost priority for either supplementing or replicating natural light. I believe strongly that you will want to choose a space where you will have access to natural light. To bring light into your sanctuary, open curtains, take down old blinds, change a light bulb, or replace the lampshade. If the room you have selected feels too "close" or confining, you could consider adding a window or skylight. You might want to add candles to any dark or shadowed areas of the room or perhaps a beautiful lamp. All of these ideas can be helpful where daylight cannot enter or where natural light is severely limited.

We rarely think about how light plays such an important part in our environment.

There are times for retreating to a dark comforting womb: on a particularly stressful day or to sleep when you are ill. For creative inspiration and generally uplifting your spirit, light is a primary ingredient.

Light can also be perceived in different ways. The "light" in your space can come from your children, your heart, and your creative thinking or activity. Just remember, your soul wants to shine. In the light, you'll find delight.

Like other processes in this book, this is an intuitive process that everyone should easily understand. The quality of light illuminating objects in your space will vary throughout the day and night. Sunlight at noon on a bright day imparts a different illumination than candlelight. The brightest and strongest light source creates the greatest contrast of values resulting from these illuminations. Also, light sources that are close to objects will impart the greatest contrast in its values (light to dark). Sometimes, the contrast of light is very interesting and you can enjoy the feeling of various light textures. Experiment with your lighting to find a harmonious balance.

Artificial Lighting

Workspace and natural light might not always be available, so you will really need to consider the type of artificial light you can use. Light bulbs with the full spectrum of light are best to imitate natural light. They are now available in fluorescent lighting for energy efficiency and, although they are more expensive initially, they offer long-term savings over the life of the bulb. Depending on your schedule, you may use your sanctuary space at night where artificial lighting will be a necessity. Too much interior artificial light creates unwanted glare. Turn off or remove offensive lighting and use a smaller lamp, such as a desk lamp or a small accent lamp.

There are two general types of artificial lighting, important in your home/work sanctuary: *Ambient lighting*—washes gently over a large area and provides general lighting in your space. A common form of ambient lighting in home/workplaces is recessed lighting with a dimmer control. Ambient lighting is good for general illumination, but will cause eye strain if you try to use it alone for tasks.

Task lighting—is focused on work surfaces and has higher levels of illumination. Task lighting should be at least 16 inches above the work surface and a baffle or shade should be used so the light bulb isn't directly visible. Another popular task lighting option is halogen or other small desk lamps. Lamps with flexible arms can be moved closer to the work or farther away when it's not needed.

Always try natural light first, supplement with artificial if necessary and, of course, energy efficient lighting is the way to go.

What To Do:

- For natural light, try to place your sanctuary space facing east for morning sun or facing west for afternoon sun.
- String up those fabulous Christmas lights. String them up on your ceiling or any place that appeals to you. Make light of any darkness in your space. See how this and other kinds of lighting changes the mood of your space.
- Use pink or rose colored light bulbs to make your skin look good.
- Hang crystal pendants in a window or somewhere it can catch the light.

ELEMENT OF TEXTURE

This element is possibly my favorite. I love seashells, with their distinctive shapes and range of individual textures. I have a display of my shell collection gathered over the years and I love to touch them and feel the various textures. They are beautiful to see and some have stories behind them that remind me of wonderful memories.

We recognize trees by the texture of their bark or see holes in the bark from insects or birds. Our mountains in the western U.S. are high, rough, and jagged and our deserts have many varieties of cacti and vegetation. In higher elevations, smoother textures can be found, as in wet moss and fallen leaves. Texture in nature can be for protection. The scales on fish provide protection without inhibiting movement. How can we incorporate interesting textures into your space? Let's examine texture and what it can do for your space.

Nature offers a treasure of texture possibilities and is easily found.

There are two approaches to using texture:

Tactile texture arouses sensory interest and an emotional response and is produced from material and structure. Tactile texture is the quality of a surface and is usually three-dimensional.

Visual textures are applied by various means to existing surfaces without making any structural changes in the surface. Repeated motifs or decorative units create patterns which can be both visual and tactile. You can easily find patterns in fabrics: stripes, tartans, plaids, polka dots, florals, and countless designs that compose patterns and create visual and tactile textures.

Check out how the fabric feels with your hand. There are wonderful velvets, fine wools, cashmere, cottons, linens, and silks. Not only are these fabrics marvelous to touch, they are all natural materials.

Lighting For Texture

Light is an important factor in any use of texture, especially tactile, and shadows play a more explicit role. The 'play' of light over textural surfaces can cast lively patterns. Try to use lighting to help create the textural environment you desire. Accent lighting is one way you can create focal points or rhythmic patterns of light and dark textures within your space. It can also emphasize your room features or highlight objects or prized possessions to expose textural qualities.

Light and shadows offer qualities of the natural environment and a welcome visual relief from hard surfaces.

What To Do:

- Try feeling the textures not just with your hands but over your face and against your cheek. What does your skin tell you about the material? Each texture should evoke a different mood, a new feeling, or a totally fresh sensation.
- Consider hanging or draping fabrics or using shawls or other materials special to you. Think about using fabrics in unusual ways. Where is it written that you can't use a tablecloth for a fabulous curtain?
- Think about hanging fabric from the ceiling or padded on a wall instead of wallpaper.
- Try looking at ways you can add accent lighting through recessed down lighting or task lighting to cast shadows, frame artwork, or emphasize more texture.
- Refer back to the section on lighting for other lighting ideas.

CHAPTER THREE: SENSES

Discover Your Physical Space

Your senses will play a large role in the way you will go about creating your sanctuary. We will begin to appreciate our senses indoors by first appreciating our senses based on our experience with the outdoors.

By having awareness of our senses, we might find there are ways to recreate outdoor sensations in our interior environments.

We need to consider all the basics: sound; smell; taste; touch; and sight.

SOUND

Sound is an interesting phenomenon. It has the power to heal and calm, to energize and uplift. It can also cause you to feel tense, irritable, and out of sorts. We have all kinds of sounds to deal with too, especially in urban lifestyles. Therefore, choose your sounds carefully. What sort of sounds do you like? Which sounds do you appreciate? Maybe, you would like a great sound system in your sanctuary to play your favorite music. Be careful with this one if it involves electricity, though (see chapter on Technology).

I play my favorite quiet-time songs on my iPod. Some are with sounds like ocean waves, birdsong, and, yes, trees rustling in the wind. Sometimes, I need complete silence because it's soothing to have no sounds at all. You might want to take a minute to think about whether you want any sounds or no sounds. Your sanctuary is a good place for music that touches your soul.

Sounds from nature, such as birds chattering away outside your window or the trees rustling in the wind, could be emanating through your sanctuary.

What To Do: ·

- Try doing without sound, a kind of "sound fast." No TV, no radio, no music, and no phone conversations. See what you can appreciate or cannot do without.
- Try eliminating conversation altogether in your special place. People don't realize how much small talk they speak just to be polite and sociable. Being silent can be a real eye opener on a much deeper level. When you stop the external chatter and noise, your mind can focus inward. You may experience insights that are unexpected and surprising.
- Search out simple sound-making equipment, like the Seven Metals Singing Bowls of Tibet.
- Try hanging a wind chime or bells in your space or hang wind chimes outside the window and appreciate the tonal qualities.
- Introduce natural sounds into your space, such as waterfalls or bubbling fountains. It would be better if they are run by solar, rather than electricity (see chapter on Technology).
- Hang a mobile to deflect negative forces with their movement, especially along a corridor or any kind of stagnant corner.
- Trees give off oxygen and cut noise from a busy street; even a small potted tree or house plant will help muffle unwanted sounds.
- Natural wool, silk, or cotton rugs or carpets also reduce noise.
- Hanging any kinds of natural fabrics and upholstery pieces will also help with noise control.
- Play instrumental music or sounds from nature to provide a place of soothing for your soul, preferably using a portable device that doesn't require electrical plugs.
- Music activates various areas within the brain. It captivates and maintains attention. Your experience can be enhanced.
- Music increases the endorphin level within the body to increase euphoric feelings; it can also calm you.

SMELL

You must not underestimate the sense of smell. It can make or break your spirit faster than you can imagine. For your sense of smell, the most desirable option is to open windows and doors and to bring in the outdoor aromas. Depending on the time of year and your location, traffic pollution and environmental conditions may prevent you from doing that. For instance, in Arizona, our summer weather is simply too hot to have our doors and windows open.

Generally, pleasant aromas arouse good feelings and happy memories and we are attracted to things that smell good. I've often heard that, if you plan to sell a house, bake homemade cookies or an apple pie and put on a pot of coffee. Why? Because it smells good and buyers will think of it as a home and associate good feelings with it. Scents and aromas in your sanctuary are important to helping you relax and feel good. How do you want your space to smell? What scents and aromas make you happy? Think of more subtle smells: the smell of the ocean, aromas in the desert after a rainstorm, or the scent of pine in a forest. It could be a smell that you love from your childhood. Take some minutes to visualize and dream of these aromas.

Nothing is more memorable than a smell. One scent can be unexpected, momentary and fleeting, yet conjure up a childhood summer beside a lake in the mountains.

- Diane Ackerman

What To Do:

- Try some wonderfully scented candles, there are so many on the market these days.
- Burning incense is a great way to have fabulous aromas. Incense will also help with the energy for clearing and re-energizing your space.
- Real flowers and plants provide natural, wonderful, and inspirational scents and aromas which can energize and clear the air. I love the smell of gardenias, paperwhites (Narcissus), roses, stargazers, lavender, jasmine, and pine; the list goes on and on.
- Potpourri is a combination of dried flower petals, such as roses, mixed with spices in an open bowl or dish. Potpourri placed around your sanctuary will provide subtle aromas.
- Essential oils are a wonderful way to add scents and aromas. They are readily available and you could make your own potpourri or natural spray to use all over your space.
- I recommend avoiding artificial or electrical plug-in types of aromas; these could be more harmful than beneficial due to their chemical content.

TASTE

Your sanctuary space should offer you the possibility of delicious tastes.

How can you taste a space? You probably won't be licking the walls, but there are ways to add the sense of taste. Think of some of your favorite flavors and how you would like to enjoy them in your space. In almost any space in my house, I can enjoy my favorite cup of tea or sneak a tiny bit of chocolate. A bowl of fresh fruit in your sanctuary will trigger the memory of the tastes and bring the added benefits of smells and beautiful colors. Now, think about what might be important to add taste in your space. Chocolate walls...mmm!

What To Do:
- Write in your journal which important tastes you would like to have in your special space.
- Have a spot to place your things of taste, be it a little table with a bowl of your favorite fruit or candy.

TOUCH

We often ignore smells, but we usually completely neglect our sense of touch altogether. For me, this is one of the most important aspects of my home. There are just so many things in my house that I love to touch. Some of my very favorite things to touch are my all-natural, unbleached cotton sheets; of course, they are especially fabulous when they are fresh from the laundry. I also love to slide into my pool and feel the perfect temperature of water surrounding my body. That feels like heaven or sanctuary to me.

Fabrics can play a big role, so consider adding some soft feeling fabrics. For example, chenille, velvet, and brushed cottons are soft to the touch. What are some of your favorite feeling fabrics? Let's work on some of your own 'touch' feelings.

The velvet and silk drapery in my bedroom as well as the feel of the smooth, beautiful sugar pine floors all add to my excitement of touch.

What To Do:
- Take a page in your journal and draw a line vertically down the middle to create two columns. At the top of one column, put "good feeling;" at the top of the other column, put "bad feeling." Go about your regular day touching all kinds of things. This can be from furniture to fabrics, from your cat or dog to a plant.
- Jot down all the things that felt good to you in the good column and all the things that felt yucky in the bad column.
- Review the list to see if there are any new insights to your touch memories.
- List fabrics you like to touch and go shopping for items made with that fabric to put in your space. Ideas: a lace doily or tablecloth or a pretty silk scarf from a local thrift store.

SIGHT

Last, but surely not least, is sight. I love the old saying: "We look but we really don't see." The truth is that we sometimes go through life in a fog. Numerous times, I've driven from work to home or vice versa and couldn't tell you anything about what I saw. Around my house, it can be days before I notice something is amiss because I wasn't paying attention to what was right in front of my eyes. Combined with our other senses, sight can affect us indirectly and directly, mentally and physically.

For instance, how we see color involves reflection and absorption of light on rods and cones in our eyes and the corresponding signals that are sent to the brain. Still, we don't just see color with our eyes; we can also feel and sense color. Here are some ways to consider your sense of sight and how it may impact your sanctuary.

The physiology of sight includes color, pattern, size and shape, and distance.

What To Do:

- Cut out pictures from magazines or draw some images of things you like and want around you.
- Pay attention to things that you really dislike or do not want in your space. Your reasons for disliking something could be hidden very deeply in your psyche. You may react to certain feelings in your life and your environment. Don't worry about them. Don't let any of it bother you. What's important here is that you don't use any of them in your sanctuary space.
- A truly healing and spiritual space should delight all your senses.

After you have given your senses quite a bit of thought, write about your insights, thoughts and ideas in your journal. You may arrive at some new thoughts after you have completed these exercises.

INTUITIVENESS

Your intuition is invisible but perhaps the most powerful sense. It is a sense of instinct, of mystery. It is often referred to as your sixth sense. You can improve your mind, body, and spirit, yet achieve much higher levels of awareness by using your intuition. Intuition is a great force and being in touch with this powerful tool can get you to your "Aha!" moments. How you feel in your gut is one of the first signs of instinct or intuition.

People have used this technique and believe it really works. You probably have used your intuition sometime in the past. Remember all the times you were thinking of someone and they called you on the phone. Or, how many times did you instinctively know who was calling you?

Intuition is real and will be your advisor, guiding you closer to your true sanctuary. Every time you use your intuition "muscle," it grows bigger and becomes stronger. Intuition is not given only to those with "psychic powers." Intuition is something that everyone has and anyone can use. Just like turning on a light bulb, you have the ability to flick the switch on your intuition. You can develop this so-called power by being aware of the little voice inside you that says "Listen to me" and trust yourself. You just have to take a quiet moment to hear it and then pay attention to it.

It is something you're born with that is literally just waiting to burst out.

What To Do:

- Believe in yourself and trust yourself.
- Your "third eye" lies between your eyebrows. Simply thinking or meditating on it can help improve awareness.
- Rely on your intuition, your "gut feeling."
- Find your true passion and purpose through your dreams.
- Make every goal you set an inevitable accomplishment and know this intuitively.
- Let quick answers and solutions flow straight into your consciousness without time-wasted efforts.
- Tap into your power of attraction which can draw people, ideas, and projects to you.
- Live a relaxed, frustration-free life with the knowledge that everything you create will have success.
- Know intuitively your results will be a success (i.e., positive thinking).
- Trust yourself 100% in every decision you make whether it's big or small.

Dreams pass into the reality of action. From the actions stem the dream again; and this interdependence produces the highest form of living.

- Anais Nin

*When something is orderly and clean,
its essence shines radiantly.*

CHAPTER FOUR: CLEANING & CLEARING

CLEANING

Cleaning is soulful work. We get down on our hands and knees. We ground ourselves as we do in gardening and connecting with the earth. By cleaning our physical environment, we realize that we are sweeping out the dust along with our old thoughts and emotions. We are also symbolically (see chapter One/Symbols & Symbolism) purifying our space of negative attitudes and feelings, allowing good energy to flow.

Once you have decided on your sanctuary space, you will need to physically clean the area. If you are building new space, clearing away debris and cleaning will be required, too. Either way, the cleaning process will include purging things that are useless, obsolete, or have little or no meaning. Getting clear, mentally and physically, about your space will allow all the good energy to enter. When things are clean, you will feel better about the process of creating. Your heart will sing and you will be able to move forward. The solution is clear: clean it out!

What To Do:

- Search around your home or work place and be on the lookout for mess and clutter, especially any area that might be used in your sanctuary space. Some areas will be quite obvious to spot. You might need to go behind the sofa and into drawers and closets.

- Once all your belongings are identified, began the amazing and soulful process of cleaning and clearing (See next section). The trick will be to keep it clean and uncluttered. You want the space to soothe your soul rather than enliven your mind.

- Stay focused. Always think about how wonderful your space will look all clean and uncluttered.

- Schedule regular times for cleaning.

- Choose cleaning products with care. Use all natural cleaning products.

- Use essential oils in your cleaning. Add a few drops on a cotton ball in the vacuum bag or a few drops on a cleaning cloth.

- Use your imagination as to scenting with essential oils. Let the oils work for you. One of my favorite formulas when cleaning is lavender scent. I use a few drops of the lavender oil mixed with water in a spray bottle and spritz the water in the air.

- Check your local health food store for other ideas using natural oils.

CLEARING

By now, you are becoming more sensitive to your space.

Now that everything is clean and uncluttered, stand in your space. Does it feel different? Usually, it will feel fabulous. I like thinking of this feeling; it's the same feeling you have when you first step out of your bath or shower. It will surely look different, even if it's only your perception.

We have another step in the cleaning and clearing process: psychic clearing. Many people all over the world respect this process and say that it works. In cultures where the concept of "vital energy" is understood, people spend as much time on psychic clearing as we do on cleaning.

For most of us, not only have we never had our homes and spaces cleared, we aren't sure what psychic clearing really is. Some of the following examples of psychic clearing might be somewhat more familiar to you.

For example: incense wafted around the church is cleansing the atmosphere; a bottle of champagne smashed against a new ship is a consecrating ritual; and, bells which ring on a Sunday morning before or after a church service. These were not intended to just call worshippers to prayer or perhaps celebrate a marriage, but also to cleanse the church sanctuary and the parishioners with the healing sound of the ringing bells.

Here is another thought on clearing. Let's say you never cleaned a space for 10 years; no dusting, no vacuuming, no window cleaning. It would pretty awful, and not very pleasant to even contemplate. Now think about everything that's happened in a space at your home or workplace over the last 10 years. You may have had some good times but you might also have had heartache, depression, anger or hopelessness. Other people might have brought their negative feelings into that room. What about the people who may have been there before you? Do you know what energy they left behind? I've lived in my house for 31 years. Think of the layers of emotional grime like sadness, jealousy, resentments and so on built up in your home or work place.

Some people have their home blessed before they move into it.

Wouldn't it be better to start fresh and build up your own personal psychic atmosphere? Even if you have just moved into a brand new home or building, space clearing is still worth your while. The building site, as well as all those who worked on it, will have left their personal emotions, moods, and energy in your space.

Even if you're not convinced, what could it hurt? There are professionals who can do this for you. If your life doesn't seem to be moving in the direction you would like, hiring an expert may be a good solution. If you don't want to hire someone, do some research on the subject and try it yourself. Trust your instincts. Keep in touch with your feelings and your intuition about your space, and you really won't go wrong.

What To Do: ·

- To begin any clearing, you must be clean. So, shower, take a bath, and be spotless in all areas of space and body.
- Try breaking up any thick and unpleasant atmosphere in a room with a party noisemaker. If there have been recent arguments in the room, it can bring a childlike innocence back into the room.
- Clapping your hands is a basic move for clearing. Move around the rooms systematically clapping into every corner, nook, and cranny. Some professional 'clearers' use bells. If you have a really pure and clear toned sounding bell, you could use it, but I suggest that you read up on the subject or inquire with a professional.
- I have also had the pleasant experience of "sageing" spaces. This requires purchasing a sage grass bundle and lighting it. Let it smoke while moving it around the area in a sweeping motion, making sure that the smoke gets into the corners. It is similar to incense, only thicker.

DE-CLUTTERING

Hanging on to things in the belief that you will one day have a use for them is a great way to clutter up your space and your spirit.

We all own stuff. The amount of stuff we own can clutter up our home or workspace, so we rent extra storage units to accommodate it all. This kind of accumulation drains our finances as well as our energy and spirit. Get rid of anything that might be negative. There is no right way to de-clutter, you just start doing it. No matter how difficult or easy it may be for you, it is essential and must be done. As you begin to clear your things out, you might notice wonderful things happening. For example, as you release more old things, you will have room to receive new things. This can be also in form of wonderful new belongings and opportunities you really do want and need. Try this also with your clothes and other items you no longer want or use.

What To Do:
- Clean off all horizontal surfaces.
- Take it in small steps; clean out one drawer at a time or just a little area or surface.
- Or, plunge in and get it over with. Way cool!
- Rid yourself of excessive or useless things.
- Make three separate piles:
    1) keep
    2) donate to a local thrift shop or charity
    3) trash

Workspace

We are now living in an era when cellular telephones and personal communication devices blur the lines between home and work. Many people are filled with anxiety over potential job loss. It is becoming more difficult than ever to be calm at work. As information overload threatens to swamp us, workplace designers are finding it more important to create spaces for employees to escape the madness, at least for brief moments of their day.

Stress doesn't always have to start at the office. It can result from the way we live our lives. The boundaries between work time and personal time are now enmeshed. The speed at which information can be retrieved and the speed at which we are expected to respond is higher than ever before. It is for this reason that office environments must include designated "downtime" spaces, such as lunch rooms, "snooze rooms," or even a place to gaze out the window for a moment and reflect. It needs to be approached holistically. Lighting (see section on Lighting) and noise play a major role in the workplace. Color can effect people's emotions in that space. Rather than being corporate, it is more about creating a comfortable workplace away from home.

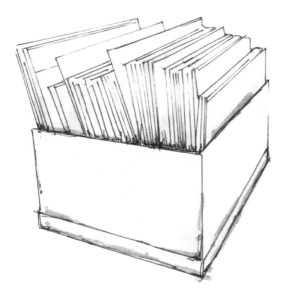

Sensory variations within a space will help us feel less like we are chained to our desks.

What To Do

- Add fabrics you might find in your home.
- Add real plants.
- Put up art, photos, and objects with meaning to the employees and the business.
- Use as much natural light and fresh air as possible.
- Give people something interesting to see within the space.

Organizing

Those piles of paperwork must be put into order. Organization and productivity are linked, but it doesn't seem to be something we're taught. Some minds work in a more organized and systematic ways if things around us are in place. The good news is that you can learn some of these skills and the best place to start is probably your desk layout.

Once your space is in order, you can consider accessorizing with plants, photos, and other things that might boost your workday experience. If you enjoy your work, then you will feel better and be more productive.

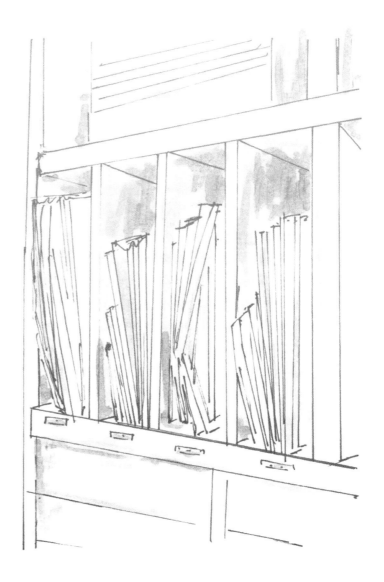

What To Do:

- Place any items used constantly within arm's reach.
- Allot a regular time for scheduling, writing notations, and any activities to organize your work time.
- Treat this time like any other appointment that can't be missed.

Privacy & Storage

In a home office that is also used as your private sanctuary, it's great to be able to hide things away when you switch out of sanctuary mode. There are many options to differentiate your office/sanctuary from the rest of your home. You can tuck things away behind screens and cabinets. If you have to share the space with someone, a privacy screen or divider is essential. If your space is severely limited, storage in desks, side desks, or a credenza become a way of sectioning off or creating privacy space and storage.

If you have to share the space with someone, a privacy screen or divider is essential.

My sister is a hair stylist. Every night, she has to pack up all of her tools, combs, and appliances and store them in a large room along with the equipment of 25 other stylists. She has to rely on locked storage to secure her belongings and special items. During working hours, she defines her workspace/sanctuary with pictures of her children and grandchildren. Sometimes, she has fresh flowers and other items of interest on display, but she changes these things regularly. When she takes a break or has some free time between appointments, she can sit in her area and look at her things, maybe even relax with a magazine.

If you have no one to answer to but yourself, it might be more difficult to clean up and store things away. You could get lazy and think: Who's going to know? At the very least, your desire to achieve this goal will instill accountability for this special space.

What To Do:
- Accountability! Be accountable for your environment.
- Storage is always good; it can be creative, multi-purpose sanctuary space.
- Develop a lighting plan to create privacy, accentuate or hide special storage areas, and define your work time and your sanctuary time.

CHAPTER FIVE: ENERGY FLOW & FENG SHUI'S CH'I

The energy in your home or work place must be able to circulate easily, to "flow". If the energy becomes stagnant or sluggish because of clutter, this will affect the sanctuary's energy flow. You're probably somewhat familiar with Feng Shui, a philosophy originally from China. Literally, Feng means "wind" and Shui means "water." It is a skill for understanding how wind and water circulate on earth. Feng Shui is a pillar of the Chinese culture and a way of life.

For the Chinese, no decision is taken without referring to the vital force or ch'i. If ch'i is blocked, you will have to enhance its energy. If there are negative influences, you will have to use devices, such as mirrors, wind chimes, and any other such remedies to create good vibes. They all agree on one thing: energy flow (ch'i) is important to make it a good space. Energy is the life force. Everything has it. Whether it is material or spiritual, it exists.

In a house where there is dust, clutter, piles of rubbish and unfinished business, all of this can affect the ch'i or energy flow.

When flow of energy is clogged, the energy stagnates. Too much action is also a possibility. Being overactive depends on what other energies are reacting with it. In other words, clutter means confusion. What we want to achieve is balance, which gives us peace. A happy and healthy space requires the balance of both Yin (at rest energy) and Yang (active energy). Yin is feminine: soft colors and fabrics or comfortable seating (rest). Yang is masculine: a water feature, fireplace, fun mobile, or wind chimes (active).

What To Do:

- The solution is clear: balance the energies.
- Make the space happy through nature; through natural solutions.
- Understand your attractions to your space. Where does it feel good? Where is that peaceful spot?
- Think of healing, restoring your vitality.
- Plan for positive energy flow.
- Have a Fung Shui practitioner help you find your best, most auspicious area of your home / work.

Workspace

Remember to keep it clean. Feng Shui consultant Elizabeth Wiggins of *Feng Shui Living* says the first step to becoming less stressed and more productive is banishing clutter. "A cluttered desk is a cluttered mind {is} the way we look at it... Then there's the placement of your desk, which ideally should see your back facing a solid wall and your eyes facing the main entrance", she says. "In a lot of offices, especially the open plan, it's not possible. You can sometimes use a high back chair or some sort of reflective item on your desk. When there are a lot of people walking behind you, you can get quite anxious". For those working from home, Wiggins says work and home should be separate where possible. One of the worst things one can do is to use the bedroom—a place of relaxation—for work.

Only a decade ago, working from home was considered unusual. Today, well over 50 million people work from home, including telecommuters and home-based businesses. Chances are, even if you're commuting to an office, you need to catch up on work at home in the evenings or on the weekends. For many, the home office is as essential as a kitchen, but the homes we live in require us to be creative in carving out our office space.

It's not just physical clutter but also your electronic clutter in your inbox, your filing system.

- Elizabeth Wiggins

What To Do:

- Surround yourself with things that only make you happy, such as holiday pictures or family photos. Use whichever personal item(s) take you to a sanctuary feeling.
- Separate your work space from your home space as much as possible.
- De-clutter: sort out your paperwork and your e-mail inbox, so your mind can follow.
- Schedule time to organize, and treat it like any other appointment that can't be missed.
- Where possible, sit with your back to a solid wall.

We need to guard ourselves by reading product labels, asking questions, and understanding the composition of items that could slowly and silently harm us.

CHAPTER SIX: TECHNOLOGY

Today's technology has given us innovations: controlled light, color theories, new products and materials, and many other revolutionary concepts. Take advantage of the many technological possibilities. Use the Internet to help you find natural products and information for your space. There is a wealth of knowledge on-line.

Whether you use high tech or more traditional methods to research and create your sanctuary, there are some things that are not good for you and your space. This includes almost anything with wiring or other electronic devices that will disturb your electromagnetic field. A field of energy surrounds each person and all living things, protecting our bodies from the exterior environment. Your electromagnetic energy can get disturbed by cell phones, computers and electrical wiring. Cell phones emit a radiation plume.

Eliminating your cell phone is probably not an option these days, because today's cell phones are much more than a telephone. They can also be your camera, video recorder, hand-held computer, GPS device, and your lifeline to staying in touch with your work and family. Try to keep them out of your sanctuary space.

There are many varieties of furnishings, finishes, and equipment which may also not be good in your sanctuary, especially for your personal health. For example, some furniture or finishes could contain contaminants, such as formaldehyde or lead, which will emit toxins over time. This is why using natural and sustainable technologies is so very important when we want to create a sanctuary.

Most cell phone headsets have a wire that can act like an antenna, and simply make matters worse. A great deal of scientific data has been suppressed by the cell phone industry and the government to protect their multi-billion dollar profits.

- Dr. Mercola

What To Do:

- Do not use anything electric, Wi-Fi, or cellular, if at all possible.
- Candles have been a natural source of artificial lighting for thousands of years. Candlelight lends a soft, golden glow and is especially appealing in an evening sanctuary space.
- No television!
- Check the chemical content of all products you are using or might wish to purchase for your sanctuary space.
- Things to avoid:
    1. anything containing lead (it is still out there)
    2. paints with low or no VOCs (volatile organic compounds)
    3. anything containing asbestos, which is very hazardous and is   known to cause cancer;
    4. products which off-gas dangerous chemicals, such as certain types of carpeting, carpet backing, some building products, some finishes on furniture and fabrics, adhesives, and sealants that can linger for years.

CHAPTER SEVEN: NATURAL ENVIRONMENTS & SUSTAINABILITY

NATURE

Natural products and materials will make your space safer and harmonious with our planet.

You may have noticed that nature or natural settings seem to be a common thread that weaves us closer to our preferred environments. There is an increasing awareness of the importance of the quality of our surroundings and environments, from recycling to "green" architecture. If you are to truly understand and develop your wellbeing and spirituality, you will need to practice this with your space. Using harmful substances or toxins will emit negative and potentially harmful energies into your space.

Many people avoid natural materials because they think they look old fashioned, are too rustic, or perhaps too expensive. There are so many new products using natural materials, you may be surprised by their innovative applications. Most are inexpensive and readily available. Some examples are the use of natural paints and varnishes derived from nature in the raw. We can use mineral products from earth like stone, slate, limestone and marble. We can borrow from the earth to make bricks, tiles, ceramics, and concrete and aggregate block. Unfortunately these also can become contaminated with radium or radon, depending on their source. Other natural products, such as, bamboo, cane, cork and grass, will make your space healthy and secure.

Natural objects are healing and alive with the energies that will provide you with a feeling of being connected. For your sanctuary space, it will be more important to welcome Mother Earth by bringing nature into your space. It is a blessing to surround yourself with the healing powers of the natural outside world. That means no plastic flowers or artificial plants because they will lack the life and the subtle energies of a living thing. Real plants are also good for the environment because they clean and clear the air. Philodendrons and English Ivy are excellent to reduce carbon pollution produced by petroleum fueled car and truck engines. Ionizers can also help clean your environment.

Fundamentally, plastics and synthetics are dead materials even if they look good and are easy to clean.

OUTDOORS

Outdoor sanctuaries have not been previously mentioned because most of us, I believe, would much rather be outside than inside. Where is your most favorite place on earth you would like to be right now? If you could be anywhere right now, this very minute, most of us would be at our favorite beach, ocean, lake, or mountain. Hardly anyone would want to be indoors if they didn't have to be. In other words, the great outdoors rules!

We don't really need a sanctuary in our outdoors because Nature is the sanctuary. Many people have sanctuaries outdoors, right in their yards or in an in-between space somewhat protected or sheltered from the elements. Gardens, outdoor shrines, altars niches, little nooks and crannies to sit and meditate are all sanctuaries. Some may have a beautiful view of the mountains or deserts. I prefer an ocean with a sandy beach where I can daydream or meditate. Others seek a shady tree, listen to the rustle of leaves and birdsong, and breathe in the earthy smells. At one time in my life, I lived in England and was fortunate to have this shade tree sanctuary. In my opinion, you are truly fortunate if you have the sound of running water from a brook or waterfall.
What a wondrous way to find sanctuary!

What To Do:
- Introduce a water feature to heal and soothe your emotions.
- Plant a tree outside your sanctuary window or place a small tree in your space. Pine trees are great for sound and privacy, as well as giving off oxygen. Philodendrons, the common leafy house plants are good for soaking up carbon dioxide and reducing noise.
- Plants will require care, will make the air healthy, and will encourage you to attend your place of sanctuary indoors or outdoors.
- Plants continuously produce oxygen in the day, indoors and out.
- Plants can also be used to increase a more relaxed feeling with color and fragrances you wish to add for your well-being.

SUSTAINABILITY

If you are a little confused about the new attention on sustainability, "green", and environmentally friendly products and buildings, you aren't alone.

These words currently "sell" and it's important to be clear exactly what these things mean. With sustainability, the key question to ask is "How long will it last?" I have heard it said that something sustainable should last at least seven generations. Generally, we want something to last, but what does that entail?

We want to do the right thing for our sanctuary as well as our planet. When addressing the sustainability issue in creating a sanctuary space, keep it simple.

What To Do:

- Make your space durable, lasting at least seven generations.
- Conserve energy.
- Read labels.
- Make healthy choices.
- Try using natural pigments (as powder or in tubes) to mix with a porous off-white paint. Use a little bit at a time until you reach your desired color.
- Try mixing beeswax with linseed oil and a little of your favorite essential oil to wax your furniture.
- Hang natural fabrics, weavings, or natural rugs to give warmth to a surrounding. They can give feelings of security and reduce noise.
- Make sure anything you have was not treated with hazardous chemicals.
- Bring in some plants for health (living energy), peace, and tranquility.
- Leave windows open for fresh air whenever possible.
- If at all possible, let natural sunlight into your environment. Options include solar tubes, clerestories, and skylights as well as windows.
- Read *Cradle to Cradle* by William McDonough.

*Create a sanctuary
where your soul feels
cared for and your
soul will pay you back
tenfold.*

- Silvianne T. Steinbach

CHAPTER EIGHT: SPIRITUALITY

SPIRITUALITY

We must act from a higher power to achieve a sanctuary. We must recognize the Divine within ourselves. Align yourself with positive energies and the Divine spirit to accomplish this place of sanctuary. We must think of loving thoughts. We must arrange our thoughts and our design elements in agreement. This will harmonize with your intentions and unleash your creative potential to a spiritual awakening.

Once this is understood, this will manifest into your sacred space which should be magical for you. Most of your effects have been in an aesthetic direction with some spiritual undertaking. At this point of your personal adventure, your responsibilities have been choices for yourself. This should be a rewarding and fulfilling experience in creating an effective design that will bring positive forces into your life. What really matters is what is in your heart, mind, body, and spirit; all connected together to bring you sanctuary. Knowing this will help you appreciate what you have created. We cannot rely on material things to be at peace. We must feel that peace in our soul. We are already whole, complete, and perfect, but we need a living environment that reflects and supports this.

A truly healing and spiritual space should delight you and make you feel blissful.

What To Do:

- Relax in your space.
- Sitting quietly, take a deep breath and meditate.
- When your mind wanders, it's okay to not have perfect attention; bring it back to your breathing.
- Focus on your breathing.
- Enjoy what you have created.
- Try to remain emotionally detached from your sanctuary space; after all, it is a reflection of you.

ALTARS & SHRINES

Almost everyone I know has some sort of altar in their home, even if it's family photos. Most often, we wish to display our trinkets and photos. This is especially meaningful in a sacred environment. Some people change them often; others keep them in the same place, never changing them. It can be interesting to others and even meaningful. Crosses, statues, and other religious icons are examples of shrines or altars. These types of symbols evoke different meanings in different cultures. Most important is what it means to you. Altars can mean being, living, projecting, and even transcending yourself. They can help your state of consciousness. They can lift your spirits. My entire home is the altar that nourishes my soul day in and day out. Hopefully, it will eventually work that way for you. If you paint the walls in a space, you might realize that the rest also needs some working, too. This is a creative process and, as the old saying goes, "Rome wasn't built in a day."

Altars are symbols of self-awareness.

What To Do:

- Display icons that nourish you.
- Be conscious about what you bring into your sanctuary, everything has its energy and everything has its effects.
- Use the sound of tingling bells to soothe your spirit.
- Choose varied elements that work with nature.
- Project your spirit and imagination into your actions.
- Follow your inner voice; you have the final say.
- Look for ways to expand your sacred space.

*No one outside of us
knows the inside of us
better than we do.*

CHAPTER NINE: SUMMARY

In order to create, you need some inspiration. Set a goal. Think of an idea or an image in your mind's eye or with the help of other images. That image or idea may not be very clear, but it must be there in order for you to create. True sanctuary happiness comes from a sense of peace and contentment within. Follow the great principles and elements of divine design. Be clean and be quiet. Work from your heart and draw from the quiet space inside you.

What To Do:
- Celebrate your victories, no matter how small they are.
- Try all the different techniques.
- Continue to look at the world around you.
- Take photos of places or spaces you'd like to create for inspiration.
- Visit places of sanctuary.
- Talk to people about their concept of sanctuary; gather ideas.
- Experiencing your space is unique to your own personal perceptions.
- This space will be part of you and it will continue to evolve, changing only to suit you.
- Continue to experiment with the space.
- Remember to laugh at yourself. Laughter helps with the creative process. The act of creating is a process.
- Allow yourself to take breaks, slow down and enjoy what you have accomplished.
- Practice patience in your life when working on your sanctuary.
- Follow your heart.
- Keep yourself healthy.
- We see, touch, hear, smell and taste. Therefore, use all of your senses and experience whatever your life is, right in this moment.
- The level of your intent is directly related to your ability to manifest your sanctuary space.
- The old adage "cleanliness is next to godliness" ring loud and clear for creating your sanctuary space.

Blessings.

Bibliography

Book References

Bevlin, Marjorie Elliott. *Design Through Discovery*, 6th Edition, Harcourt Brace & Company, 1994

Colin, Terah Kathryn. *The Western Guide to Feng Shui*, Hay House, Carlsbad, CA 1996

Cooper, David. *Simplicity and Solitude*, Bell Tower, New York, 1992

Day, Christopher. *Places of the Soul*, Thorsons, London, 1990

Fairchild, Dennis. *Healing Homes*, Wave Field Books, Birmingham, MI, 1996

Gimbel, Theo. *The Book of Color Healing*, Gaia, London, 1994

Goldman, Jonathan. *Healing Sound*, Shaftesbury, England, 1992

Khalsa, Jagatjoti S. *Altar Your Space*, Mandala Publishing, www.mandala.org

Kingston, Karen. *Creating Sacred Space with Feng Shui*, Broadway Books, New York, 1997

Kopec, Dak. Health, *Sustainability, and the Built Environment*, Fairchild Books, Inc. 2009

Linn, Denise. *Sacred Space*, Rider, London, 1995

Logan, Karen. *Clean House Clean Planet*, Pocket Book, New York, 1993

Meyer, Laurine Morrison. *Sacred Home*, Llewllyn Publication, 2004

Pagram, Beverly. *Natural Housekeeping*, Gala, London, 1997

Rossbach, Sarah & Yum, Lin. *Living Color*, Kodansha International, New York, 1994

St. James, Elaine. *Simplify Your Life,* Hyperion, New York, 1994

Streep, Meg. *Alters Made Easy*, Harper Collins Publishers, 1997

Magazine and Journal Articles References

Ahrentzen, S.B."Home as a Workplace in the Lives of Women", In l. Altman & S. Low (Eds.), Place attachment: *Human Behavior and Environment*, (vol. 12 pp 113-138), New York Plenum Press (1992)

A.V.N. "Cut the Clutter", *Yoga Journal,* p.21, Sept/Oct (2004)

Baxter, Kathleen. "A Sanctuary for Watercolor", *American Artist*, no700, p66-71, Nov. (2000)

Berke, Debra. "The Challenges and Rewards of Home-Based Self Employment", *Journal of Family Issues*, Vol.24, no4, p513-546, May (2003)

Bertelsen, Ann; Cohoon, Sharon Whiteley, Peter O Lorton, Steven R Bowling, Mary Jo. "Backyard Retreats", *Sunset*, no.6, p106-118, 208, Jun (2002)

Boyd, Sarah. "Intimate Horizon: Making the Bedroom a Sanctuary", *Essence* , v24 n1 p124(4), May 1993

Breathnach, Sarah Ban. "Home Is Where My Heart Is", *Good Housekeeping*, v226 n6 p78(1) May (1998)

Doyle, Alice. "Offering for a Simple Sanctuary", *Southern Living*, no 1, p61, Jan. (2002)

Griswold, Mac. "A History of the Sanctuary Garden", *Design Quarterly*, n169 p2, (31), summer (1996)

Gumper, Gary and Drucker, Susan. "The Mediated Home in the Global Village", *Communication Research*, v25n4 p422, (17) Aug. (1998)

Hettinger, Mary Ellen. "Peaceful Places", *Your Health*, p.30-32, Sept. (1990)

Lasky, Julie. "House of the Spirit", *Interiors*, v158 i12 p8, Dec. (1999)

Mulrine, Anna. "City Sanctuaries", *US News & World Report*, p47, Dec. 3, (1999)

Oliver, Julie. "Inner Sanctum", *Houses*, 26(5), Nov (2001)

Schaub, Charlyne Varkonyi. "'02Trends: Comfy Styles Cushions Blow to Psyches", *Orlando Sentinel.* The (Fl), Edition: Metro, Section: Homes pJ1, January 6, (2006)

Stoddard, Alexandra. "Style: Keep It Pure and Simple", *McCall's,* , Living Beautifully, p126, Aug. (1990)

Tomasulo, Katy. "The Great Escape", *Builder*, p120-123, Mar.(2002)

Web Sites References

http://www.google.com/search?sourceid=gmail&rls=m&q=Electromagnetic%20 fields, Google (accessed on 10/27/2009)

www.invisible (accessed 10/01)

www.live-to-fish.cn/439729-A-Place-of-Sanctuary-Creating-Sanctuary-Creating-Sacred-Space.html

www.live- to-fish.cn (accessed on 10/27/09)

www.drmercola.com (accessed natural health blog, daily, 2009-2010)

www.WilliamMcdonough.com (accessed on 12/11/09)

http://www.wddty.com/your healthy house home a low pollution sanctuary.html

www.wddty.com (accessed on 11/6/2009)

Made in the USA
Charleston, SC
13 October 2010